FAITH

COMMANDER

LIVING FIVE VALUES FROM THE PARABLES OF JESUS

KORIE ROBERTSON & CHRYS HOWARD

ZONDERVAN

Faith Commander
Copyright © 2014 by Korie Robertson and Chrys Howard

This title is also available as a Zondervan ebook.
Visit www.zondervan.com/ebooks.

Requests for information should be addressed to:
Zondervan, 3900 *Sparks Dr. SE, Grand Rapids, MI 49546*

ISBN 978-0-310-82033-8

Cover design: Grey Matter Group
Cover photography: Russell A. Graves
Interior design: David Conn

Printed in the United States of America

14 15 16 17 18 19 20 21 22 23 /DCI/ 20 19 18 17 16 15 14 13 12 11 10 9 8 7 6 5 4 3 2 1

CONTENTS

ACKNOWLEDGMENTS

We would like to thank our friend and children's minister, LinDee Loveland, for her incredible contribution to *Willie's Redneck Rodeo*. She is a bottomless pit of great ideas and blesses our lives every day. Our children love Miss LinDee and we do too!

We would also like to thank Karen Lee-Thorp and Cindy Bultema. What a blessing to have such talented women help us on the *Faith Commander* adult and teen books (Karen), and children's curriculum (Cindy). They caught the vision and ran with it. You both are amazing!

A special thank you to the video crew, T. J. Rathbun, Jay Irwin, and John Pottenger, who came to Louisiana to capture who the Robertsons really are.

And to Alan, Jase, Willie, Jep, Si, Phil, Reed, John Luke, Sadie, Cole, and Will who took time out of their busy lives to lend a voice to this project. You guys are awesome men of God, and Sadie, you're an awesome God-girl!

Thank you, John Raymond, for your faith in this project and for your desire to "get it right" for the sake of the adults and children who we pray will be blessed by it. You and your entire team have been amazing to work with. We couldn't have asked for a better experience.

FIVE GREAT STORIES

We love a good story. In the Robertson family, about the time you start learning to tie your shoes is when you start listening to good stories. Later you get your chance to tell a good story. Our stories involve experiences we have gone through, taken from the ordinary things we deal with every day, but often made bigger than life to make them more fun. There may also be some surprise twists to keep you guessing. But the secret to a really good story is that it will have a point that will stay with you for the rest of your life.

It's no surprise, then, that we love Jesus's stories. He called them *parables*, which means they compare something to something else. Parables aim straight for the heart and can change yours if you let them. Think of a parable as an earthly story with a heavenly meaning from our Faith Commander: Jesus.

In this book we're going to look at five of Jesus's parables. We're going to peel them back so you can feel how outrageous they were when Jesus first told them. Then we're going to dig deep into what they tell us about how to live. Each parable deals with a value that is foundational to the way our family lives: faith, forgiveness, prayer, obedience, and kindness. Willie and I (Korie) both come from big families, and these five values are some of the main things that hold our families together. We'll be telling some true stories about the Robertson family to show you how we try to live these values.

If you've heard these parables before, we hope you'll let them hit you fresh. And if you've never heard them before, you're in for a treat. Not even Si can tell a better story than Jesus.

CHAPTER 1

REDONKULOUS FAITH

My (Korie's) in-laws, Miss Kay and Phil, set an example of faith that never stops amazing me. They got married when Miss Kay was just sixteen and Phil was seventeen. He headed off to Louisiana Tech University on a football scholarship, and she went with him. Being young was hard enough, but it was the 1960s, and college introduced Phil to drinking and drugs. When he was drunk he was angry, and Miss Kay was scared.

Their baby Alan was born, then Jase, then Willie. Phil kept drinking. In his twenties, Phil came to own a beer joint, and Miss Kay was a barmaid who didn't drink, fighting for her marriage while Phil's behavior went out of control.

A man with a Bible came to see Phil at the bar, and Phil ran him off. Miss Kay, though, decided to entrust her life to God as things with Phil went from bad to worse. She told her boys, "That's not your daddy. That's the devil in your daddy."

Phil got into a barroom brawl and fled to the woods to escape the law. Later he actually made Miss Kay and her boys move out of the family house because he said they were cramping his lifestyle. But Phil was miserable and wanted a way out of the drinking and anger. Eventually he took Miss Kay's advice and sat down with the Bible-carrying pastor who had visited his bar.

"Phil, what do you think the gospel is?" the pastor asked.

"I don't know," Phil said, "gospel music on the radio?"

The pastor explained to him how Jesus was born of a virgin, died on the cross, was buried, and was raised from the dead. Phil was blown away by the idea that Jesus died for him and was raised. They were sitting in the baptistery of the church, and Phil said, "I'm going to make Jesus the Lord of my life. I want to follow him from this day forward."

Miss Kay and the three boys were downstairs in the church, and they heard what Phil said. When Phil was baptized, the boys began hollering and shouting, "My daddy's saved! My daddy's saved!"

Phil was saved—and in another way, the whole family was saved from the consequences of Phil's old life.

It took a strength of faith that Mom and I call *redonkulous* for Miss Kay to hold onto her marriage for years until Phil took that step. It took a tiny seed of redonkulous faith for Phil to believe that the gospel of Jesus was reliable to set the direction of his new life. Phil trusted that what he'd learned about Jesus was true, and as he began to act on it, his faith grew.

I love this story because it shows me how a tiny bit of real redonkulous faith can change everything. My life, and my husband Willie's life, would be so different today if Miss Kay hadn't hung onto God and if Phil hadn't taken that first step.

Faith is the number-one value our family seeks to live by. *Faith* isn't just a church word; you and I use faith many times a day in the most ordinary situations. For instance, Miss Kay loves to cook, and when she cooks she follows a recipe. She has used her recipes over and over, and she has faith that when she puts all the ingredients together, the recipe will work. Even more, if she gets a new recipe from a friend, the first time she uses it she really has to have faith that the end result will taste good! Faith simply means *trusting* that something or someone is true or reliable, and *acting* on the basis of that trust.

God sometimes works through "recipes" we're familiar with. When he sends the normal amount of rainfall for our area, things happen the way we expect. When we drop something, we expect it to hit the ground because God's "recipe" for gravity is reliable. When we've seen God do something for us over and over, that familiar knowledge makes our faith strong in that area.

On the other hand, new things often happen to us. Too much rain, or too little. The loss of a job. A new baby. Whether we see them as good or bad, unfamiliar events stretch our faith. Can God handle it? Do we want God to be God in this situation, or do we want to write our own recipe?

The other values our family lives by all depend on faith in God—on trusting God to be God in our situation. We can't be consistently kind and forgiving to broken human beings just by trying hard. No, to be kind and forgiving we need faith that is redonkulously strong, redonkulously trusting, no matter what happens.

THE PARABLE OF THE SOWER

When Jesus wanted to explain redonkulous faith to farmers, He told a parable about four kinds of soil. He told it to a crowd and then explained it to His disciples:

That same day Jesus went out of the house and sat by the lake. Such large crowds gathered around him that he got into a boat and sat in it, while all the people stood on the shore. Then he told them many things in parables, saying: "A farmer went out to sow his seed. As he was scattering the seed, some fell along the path, and the birds came and ate it up. Some fell on rocky places, where it did not have much soil. It sprang up quickly, because the soil was shallow. But when the sun came up, the plants were scorched, and they withered because they had no root. Other seed fell among thorns, which grew up and choked the plants. Still other seed fell on good soil, where it produced a crop—a hundred, sixty or thirty times what was sown. Whoever has ears, let them hear."

The disciples came to him and asked, "Why do you speak to the people in parables?"

He replied, "Because the knowledge of the secrets of the kingdom of heaven has been given to you, but not to them. Whoever has will be given more, and they will have an abundance. Whoever does not have, even what they have will be taken from them. This is why I speak to them in parables: Though seeing, they do not see; though hearing, they do not hear or understand.

"In them is fulfilled the prophecy of Isaiah:

"'You will be ever hearing but never understanding;
　　you will be ever seeing but never perceiving.
For this people's heart has become calloused;
　　they hardly hear with their ears,

and they have closed their eyes.
Otherwise they might see with their eyes,
    hear with their ears,
understand with their hearts
    and turn, and I would heal them.'

"But blessed are your eyes because they see, and your ears because they hear. For truly I tell you, many prophets and righteous people longed to see what you see but did not see it, and to hear what you hear but did not hear it.

"Listen then to what the parable of the sower means: When anyone hears the message about the kingdom and does not understand it, the evil one comes and snatches away what was sown in their heart. This is the seed sown along the path. The seed falling on rocky ground refers to someone who hears the word and at once receives it with joy. But since they have no root, they last only a short time. When trouble or persecution comes because of the word, they quickly fall away. The seed falling among the thorns refers to someone who hears the word, but the worries of this life and the deceitfulness of wealth choke the word, making it unfruitful. But the seed falling on good soil refers to someone who hears the word and understands it. This is the one who produces a crop, yielding a hundred, sixty or thirty times what was sown."

(Matthew 13:1–23)

I (Chrys) am fascinated by the way this parable is rooted in the everyday lives of the people Jesus was talking to. In the first century, farmland might be miles away from the farmer's home, so this farmer went some distance to his field and began to sow his seed. He had already plowed it, and now he scattered handfuls of seed on the plowed earth. Later he would plow it again, crosswise, to cover the seed with one to three inches of soil.

His technique wasn't scientific. Some of his seed fell on the hard footpaths that surrounded his field. There was no possibility that this seed would sprout: the earth was packed down hard by foot traffic and the birds quickly ate the seed.

Parts of the farmer's field were rocky with only a thin layer of soil. In other parts, thorny weeds—some grew as tall as a horse in that part of the world—were tougher than the tender crop seedlings. If you've ever tried to grow a garden in poor soil, you know what he was up against.

Happily, he did have some good soil where the seed not only sprouted but flourished. A hundredfold was an excellent harvest and represented God's blessing. It reminds us of Genesis 26:12, which says, "Isaac planted crops in that land and the same year reaped a hundredfold, because the LORD blessed him."

FANS OF THE JESUS SHOW

Jesus told this story to make a point about the different ways people responded to His message. He told it to the crowds who were following Him everywhere. Our family has learned a few things about what it's like to be a celebrity with fans showing up in front of your house at all times of the day and night. When you have a beard as Jesus had, just putting on dark glasses doesn't fool anybody! They know it's you, and they want to connect with you. Jesus had mixed feelings about the crowds. On the one hand, they disappointed Him, because most of them just wanted to see the Jesus Show and didn't want to do anything about what He was saying. On the other hand, each one of them was a human being, precious in the sight of God. He was glad to die for any one of them.

He told this Parable of the Four Soils to help them think about which kind of soil they were. To put it another way, you might say He was trying to sort the fresh fish from the rotten fish — and from the in-between fish that don't yet smell bad but soon will.

The first group of people in the crowd was like a path made of hard-packed earth. Their hearts were like a working man's hands with calluses on them. Nothing Jesus said or did was going to soak in. They didn't want the real God to exist. They didn't want God to be God. They might be religious, but they didn't want the actual God to meddle in their lives. In fact, the scariest thing was that every time these people heard Jesus teach something, they pushed it away and their hearts got a little harder. His teaching irritated them. It made them uncomfortable. They were tuning in to the Jesus Show mostly to make fun of Him. Doing that made them feel better about themselves.

The second group in the crowd was like the rocky soil. If the first group had hard hearts, this group had shallow hearts. From their first reaction to the Jesus Show, you'd think they were committed followers, ready to salute and do what Jesus said. But they were only fans. They were happy to wear the hat and the T-shirt, but as soon as following Jesus started to make them unpopular, they were going to disappear like frogs jumping into the river.

The third group wasn't so much scared of persecution as they were distracted. The thorn bushes of the world — things they owned or wanted to own, things they were expected to do, and the messages coming at them from other people—all that was choking the life out of them. The Greek noun behind the word *deceitfulness* is *apate*, which can mean either deception or pleasure. Material things offer pleasure, but it can be a deceptive pleasure.

Church buildings are sometimes full of these distracted people. They go to church and sing songs, but they have no real faith in Christ. They treat the church like a social club. They're more worried about created things rather than the Creator.

Jesus wasn't doing His ministry for the distracted, the fans, or the critics. He was doing it for the fourth group: the genuine disciples. These were the people who heard His teaching, understood it, and bore the fruit of changed lives. They made it all worthwhile. By hearing and responding, these people were gradually softening their hearts to hear and understand more and more. They might not understand much in the beginning, but they did something with what little they understood, so the seed sprouted and grew and produced a crop.

BELIEF PLUS SURRENDER PLUS ACTION

The response Jesus wanted was faith. Wherever we see the words *faith* or *believe* in the New Testament, they are usually a translation from the original Greek root word *pistis*. The noun form of *pistis* is usually translated as "faith" and the verb form, *pisteuo*, is translated as "believe." *Pistis* can also mean "faithfulness," and redonkulous faith has an element of faithfulness in it. It isn't just theoretical belief. It includes trust, surrender, and faithfully acting on the basis of the belief.

Faith simply means trusting that something or someone is

true or reliable, and acting on the basis of that trust. It means making choices consistent with that belief.

Jesus is happy if you start with just a tiny amount of faith, as long as that faith is genuine. In another parable, He compares faith to a mustard seed (Matthew 13:31–32). Mustard seeds are the tiny round seeds of various mustard plants and are usually about one or two millimeters in diameter, or about one-twentieth of an inch.

Redonkulous faith can be as tiny as a mustard seed, but it's as powerful as a mighty wind. It trusts that God is our defender, deliverer, and provider. Actions like forgiveness and kindness and obedience flow naturally from redonkulous faith. But without redonkulous faith, it's hard to keep forgiving people when they're harsh, keep being kind when they're cold, keep obeying God when He asks difficult things. You just run out of gas.

If you want to see redonkulous faith in action, read chapter 11 of the book of Hebrews, and flip back to the Old Testament to read the stories of the people listed in Hebrews. For instance, God told Abraham,

> "Go from your country, your people and your
> father's household to the land I will show you.
> "I will make you into a great nation,
>   and I will bless you;
> I will make your name great,
>   and you will be a blessing.
> I will bless those who bless you,
>   and whoever curses you I will curse;
> and all peoples on earth
>   will be blessed through you."

(Genesis 12:1–3)

Abraham obeyed God's command to leave his country and his family to go to a distant land because he had faith in God and His promises. He didn't live long enough to see God make his descendants into a great nation, or to see all peoples on earth blessed through him, but he had confidence in what he didn't see because he had faith in God. The writer of Hebrews says, "faith is confidence in what we hope for and assurance about what we do not see" (Hebrews 11:1).

WHAT WE BELIEVE

What things that we don't see does God want us to have assurance about? Well, first of all, God wants us to believe He exists even though we don't see Him. He also wants us to have confidence that He has done some important things. He wants us to be confident that Jesus came to earth as God in human form at a particular time in history at a particular place in the world. Jesus lived a perfect life and then died on the cross for the sins of the world. He was buried and then rose from the dead to prove that He had triumphed over death. He now sits at the right hand of God the Father to mediate for those who have put their faith in Him. God asks us to believe the evidence in the Bible that these things really happened in history and that Jesus is alive now, active on our behalf.

We don't believe these things blindly, without evidence. But we do have to trust the reliability of the evidence. One source of evidence is the Bible, which tells us about God's acts in history. We also have the evidence of God's existence in the world around us. If you live in a city where everything around you seems to be made by human beings, you can lose touch with the evidence of the natural world. But if you spend your life out fishing on the river or hunting in the woods, you feel that evidence everywhere around you. Jase told us,

> My first God experience, after witnessing the transformation in my parents' lives, was actually out in the woods. I was hunting, I looked around, and I remember just stopping everything and thinking, "Somebody built this. This earth is just too incredible to come from nothing." And so the seeds of God were planted basically on the observation of His creation. I thought, "This has a design and it demands a designer." And the more I began to reflect on that, and think about that, and ask questions about that, the more spiritual conversations I started having, and through that I was led to hearing the message of Jesus Christ and what He did for not only my sins, but for the hope of me living forever.

So we have the evidence of the Bible and the evidence of the natural world. We also have the evidence of what God does in people here and now, like the way Phil transformed before his family's eyes after he decided to follow Jesus. People like Phil don't change that much without some powerful influence.

Jase told us a funny story about how he experienced change in his own life. He wasn't a bad kid who needed to clean up his life in obvious ways, but he was a shy kid. At fourteen years old he put his faith in Jesus Christ, and he wanted to tell people about his faith, but when he went to school or out in public, he was too nervous to speak. Then one night he got done praying about being more vocal about his faith, and about midnight his land line phone rang. He answered it, but the other person didn't speak. He said, "Hello? Hello?" but the caller remained silent.

Jase knew it might be a prank caller, and he was getting ready to hang up, but then he realized something. He said, "You know what? I'm glad you called, because I've been wanting to share my faith in Christ, and I've been unable to do it in public because I'm shy. So I'm going to share with you what I'm in on." Jase started right there and introduced this unknown caller to Jesus Christ.

After ten or fifteen minutes he tried again to get the caller to say something, but no luck. He could hear that someone was there, though. He heard pages rustling and assumed the caller was following along in the Bible.

This Bible study went on for three hours. Jase finally ran out of material and said, "Look, I'm sleepy. But I appreciate you calling—I feel good about this—so why don't you call back tomorrow night, same time?"

Lo and behold, the next night at midnight the person called again and sat there silent. So Jase put in another three hours. He noticed that when the person on the other end of the phone doesn't respond, you can really share what you know. After about three hours, Jase heard an outcry of emotion, and the caller hung up.

From the cry, he realized the caller was a woman. He also realized that an introduction to Jesus Christ is the most powerful message you can share with someone on this earth. What else could have held someone's attention for six hours?

After that moment, Jase knew that the message of Christ is real. It's not just something he believes because he grew up in it. What Christ represents through His death, His resurrection, and His work at the right hand of God on behalf of humanity is powerful, captivating, and real. When Jase shared his faith, it became fully real to him.

From then on, Jase shared Jesus Christ with everyone in earshot. He sat down and made a list of his friends and family, and he systematically went down that list. It was over a hundred names. He said to himself, "I'm going to approach this person, I'm going to ask if I can share my faith, and I'm going to do it." And he did. That's faith in action.

SOIL AMENDMENT

Jesus's disciples asked Him, "Increase our faith!"

He answered, "If you have faith as small as a mustard seed, you can say to this mulberry tree, 'Be uprooted and planted in the sea,' and it will obey you" (Luke 17:5–6).

Apparently, the size of your faith is less important than its quality and what you're doing with it. Are you using the faith you have?

In our family, life hasn't always been easy, so we've needed to step out in faith day after day. Miss Kay remembers what it was like in the early years of the Duck Commander® business:

> What are the odds that Jesus just happened to pick four fishermen as the first of twelve disciples?... Since our family commercial-fished the Ouachita River for the first fifteen years of the Duck Commander business, I think I understand why Jesus chose a third of His group from that profession. Fishing is very much a faith-based business. To keep going out and hoping, and sometimes praying, that those fish moved and swam into your nets really does test your faith. We spent many a morning on our knees on the riverbank praying for a good haul to pay important bills.[1]

---

1 Excerpted from *The Duck Commander Devotional* (p. 224) by permission of Howard Books.

Praying is a great way to start putting your faith into action. So is fishing!

Remember that Jesus says, "Whoever has ears, let them hear" and "Whoever has will be given more, and they will have an abundance" (Matthew 13:9, 12). What matters is using the ears you have to hear Jesus and then *responding to Him in action*. If you do that, then your hearing, responding, and believing will grow.

So here are some practical things you can do to grow in faith:

Open your ears. Listen to what Jesus is saying. Think about the parable. Which kind of soil are you? Use your ears throughout the day to hear how Jesus's words interplay with your life.

Deal with your distractions. If "the worries of this life" or "the deceitfulness of wealth" are thorns choking the fruitfulness of Jesus's word in your life, you're not doomed to be thorny soil forever. With His help you can cut down the weeds. For example, take a hard look at what possessions mean to you. Do you find your identity in the things you own? Do possessions make you feel important? Do they make you feel safe in a risky world? The Robertson family used to be poor, and now we're rich, but we don't look to money for our identity, our sense of importance, or our security. Wealth is fleeting. It comes and goes. If we found our identity in wealth or fame, then being in a TV show would have torn our family apart (as some members of the television crew warned us it would do). It's done that to other families. Don't let your faith and family be torn apart because you're chasing money.

Another way to deal with distractions is to take screen

Sabbaths. If you're connected to the world all day every day through your phone, your computer, your TV, then it might be good for your soul to spend one day every month with all the screens off. Turn off the phone, the TV, the computer, the iPod. Tell people you're going to be offline. If you can't imagine doing that, then start with maybe eight daytime hours: 8:00 a.m. to 4:00 p.m. on a Sunday once a month. Work your way up to twenty-four hours. You'll hear Jesus a lot better if your ears aren't always plugged with earbuds.

Share what you know. Jase shared his faith, and it became more real to him. If you tell someone else, your faith will get stronger.

Expect suffering. If you tend toward rocky soil, you could be under the mistaken belief that life should always feel good if you're on God's team. But Peter says,

> Dear friends, do not be surprised at the fiery ordeal that has come on you to test you, as though something strange were happening to you. But rejoice inasmuch as you participate in the sufferings of Christ, so that you may be overjoyed when his glory is revealed. If you are insulted because of the name of Christ, you are blessed, for the Spirit of glory and of God rests on you.
>
> (1 Peter 4:12–14)

Don't be surprised when suffering happens. Expect it as part of normal life. Painful experiences aren't evidence that there is no God, or that God isn't powerful or wise or good enough to make life go well. He has purposes in your suffering that we can only guess at. One of those purposes is to help your faith grow.

Address cynicism. One of the most common responses to

life in our world today is cynicism. To be cool is to have an attitude that you've seen it all and you're not impressed. That nobody can truly be trusted and you're on your own. Some people absorb this attitude from the world around them, and many have an extra dose of it because they've been let down badly somewhere along the way. Has life disappointed you? Has someone hurt you or others you care about? Are you blaming God, or have you given up believing in Him? Those are signs of calluses on your soul. You can soften them by forgiving those who have hurt you and by letting go of blaming God.

Address the things that control you. Calluses can also form on your soul if you simply don't want God to exist. Think about that. Would it get in your way if there was a God with opinions about how you live your life? If so, it's convenient to disbelieve in him. Mighty convenient. Fill in the blank in this sentence:

If God were real, then I would have to give up

_____.

The thing you put in that blank may be highly desirable, but if it makes you unable to want God to be God, then it's poisoning your life. Nothing is worth that.

Make time to worship God. Faith in God grows when we choose to worship God as God. Worshiping is saying with your whole self, "God, you deserve to be God. I'm not god of my life, and neither is anything else." If you choose to truly worship with others, your faith will get stronger.

Don't rely on feelings. Faith can't depend on feelings, because feelings come and go depending on how much sleep you got last night and whether you're hungry and what your spouse said to you this morning. Some people have strong feelings, and others hardly notice their feelings. It's okay to be either type of person, as long as you know what to do with a feeling. What to do is this: notice it. Give it some air time to talk to you. Hear it out. Is it mad? Scared? Bored? Hopeful? Happy, happy, happy? Once your feeling has had its say, decide what to do with the information. Think of your feeling as a six-year-old child: you want to listen to it, and then you need to be the faith-filled grown-up who decides what to do. If you're a good parent, you don't muzzle the child, but you also don't let him or her rule the home.

Another reason why faith can't depend on feelings is that you won't always feel God's presence. He's there all the time, but He decides whether to let you feel Him there. Sometimes He'll build your faith muscles by switching off the feelings and asking you to trust what you know to be true about Him.

Don't coast on the faith of other people. As Willie says, "Our relationship with God is personal. I've had many godly role models in life, but I had to choose for myself to put my faith in Jesus. Even though I had great parents who loved God, I could not rely on their faith."[2] We need other people to support us in faith, but we can't expect them to carry us while we coast.

GOD IN OUR DNA

When we put our trust in Jesus Christ, we become part of His family. John says this in his gospel:

---

2 Excerpted from *The Duck Commander Devotional* (p. 130) by permission of Howard Books.

Yet to all who did receive him, to those who believed in his name, he gave the right to become children of God—children born not of natural descent, nor of human decision or a husband's will, but born of God.

(John 1:12–13)

Si tells an outrageous story to illustrate this new birth:

One day I had to give blood to check and see if I had a hereditary illness. After the doctor reviewed the test results, he actually showed me my DNA. There were two strands: my mother's and my father's. After checking them all, he said I was clear of the disease. Of course I was relieved, but I told the doc that he was one strand shy. "That's crazy!" he said. "You don't know what you're talking about." But I said, "You are the crazy one, Jack! There's one more strand in there, and it's the most important one of all!" I told him the strand he was missing was the blood of Jesus Christ, because that was part of my DNA, as well.[3]

Is God part of your DNA by faith? If He isn't, now is a good time to change that! Like with Phil, it all starts with just a tiny seed of faith that God really is who the Bible says He is.

---

3 Excerpted from *The Duck Commander Devotional* (p. 39) by permission of Howard Books.

CHAPTER 2

RADICAL FORGIVENESS

My (Korie's) brother-in-law Jep is the youngest of the four Robertson sons. He was always a pretty good kid who never got into much trouble. But when he turned eighteen, he started hanging around with the wrong group of guys. Even though Jep had never been around drugs and drinking, and he knew better than to get involved in those things, he began to make poor choices. He confesses now that he figured he was a man and wanted to experiment. Before he knew it, he was involved pretty seriously in drugs and alcohol. His weight dropped to 130 pounds because he was putting all kinds of things into his body other than food.

He knew he had a problem when he woke up one night with one foot in his truck and the rest of his body hanging out the door. But sometimes, even when we can see how deep we are in sin, we can't figure out how to get out. He was worried that if he told his family, they would be disappointed in him, so he continued to be untruthful about where he was and who he was with.

One day he found a note on his truck from Willie that said, "I know what you've been up to. We need to talk." At that point all Jep could think was, "Oh no." He didn't call Willie back right then, but a few days later, he went to his parents' house and saw all of his brothers' trucks parked there.

He walked in, and there sat his dad and all his brothers. Phil said, "We know what you've been up to. You got two choices, son. You can find someplace else to work and live while you wreck your life with drinking and drugs, or you can do what it's going to take to quit this stuff."

Jep fell on his knees crying and said, "What took y'all so long?"

To his surprise, nobody got mad at him for what he was doing. Nobody made him feel worse than he already felt or made him pay for the heartache and humiliation he'd caused. Instead, they cried and hugged him. Phil put him on three months of house arrest to keep him away from bad friends and temptation, and every day Phil and Jep studied the Bible together and went hunting to keep Jep occupied and on track while he was getting sober.

For Alan, that morning was one of maybe three times in his adult life when he has cried openly. The reason Alan— and Phil—cried and easily forgave Jep instead of shouting and blaming him was that Alan and Phil had been in that same place in the past. When Alan was seventeen, his life took a wrong course, and through many bad choices he nearly lost his family and even his own life. Phil and Miss

Kay forgave Alan for the harm he'd done to the family, so Alan was more than happy to offer Jep that same forgiveness.

It's important for everyone to know that the Robertsons are just a normal family with normal flaws and imperfections. Life is hard, and getting along with others is definitely one of life's greatest challenges. But Scripture tells us clearly to "live in peace." Knowing how hard it is to get along with coworkers, many people have asked us how we all work together and still enjoy being with each other. There's no secret to how this works. It's all right there in the Bible.

Jesus laid out a way of life for His followers that was "upside down" from the way the rest of the world lived at the time He walked the earth and still is today. Forgiving other people who have wronged us or hurt us or embarrassed us is not easy. In fact, sometimes it seems impossible. But that is what God did for us and what He asks us to do for others. When we've experienced that kind of radical, extreme forgiveness, then forgiving others suddenly makes all the sense in the world.

SEVENTY-SEVEN MILLION TIMES

One day Jesus's right-hand man, Peter, went to Jesus to have this whole forgiveness thing spelled out for him. Peter said, "Lord, how many times shall I forgive my brother or sister who sins against me? Up to seven times?"

Seven seemed like a generous number to Peter. If somebody does the same thing to you over and over, you might put up with it once or twice, but after seven times surely you get a pass to stop trying.

But Jesus said, "I tell you, not seven times, but seventy-seven times."

What? Peter's jaw probably hung open like a dead fish when he heard that. He was likely thinking about the people in his life who were smart enough to know just how far they could take advantage of his good side. If selfish people know they can mess with you seventy-seven times and you'll forgive them, you would think it would be safe to conclude that they might take advantage of the situation. Right?

But Jesus had more to say on this subject. He said "seventy-seven times" as a way of conveying, "Don't keep score. Just keep forgiving them. A million times if you have to."

Why did Jesus say this? Why does this crazy course of action make sense? Jesus told a parable to explain why. It's called the Parable of the Unmerciful Servant.

A TALE OF TWO DEBTS

Here's the parable:

> "Therefore, the kingdom of heaven is like a king who wanted to settle accounts with his servants. As he began the settlement, a man who owed him ten thousand bags of gold was brought to him. Since he was not able to pay, the master ordered that he and his wife and his children and all that he had be sold to repay the debt.
>
> "At this the servant fell on his knees before him. 'Be patient with me,' he begged, 'and I will pay back everything.' The servant's master took pity on him, canceled the debt and let him go.
>
> "But when that servant went out, he found one of his fellow servants who owed him a hundred silver coins. He

grabbed him and began to choke him. 'Pay back what you owe me!' he demanded.

"His fellow servant fell to his knees and begged him, 'Be patient with me, and I will pay it back.'

"But he refused. Instead, he went off and had the man thrown into prison until he could pay the debt. When the other servants saw what had happened, they were outraged and went and told their master everything that had happened.

"Then the master called the servant in. 'You wicked servant,' he said, 'I canceled all that debt of yours because you begged me to. Shouldn't you have had mercy on your fellow servant just as I had on you?' In anger his master handed him over to the jailers to be tortured, until he should pay back all he owed.

"This is how my heavenly Father will treat each of you unless you forgive your brother or sister from your heart."

(Matthew 18:23–35)

We start with a king, the sort of king who was common in Jesus's day. One of the king's servants owed him ten thousand "bags of gold." In the original language Jesus gave a precise weight of each "bag of gold," enough to pay a worker minimum wage for *twenty years*. Each bag. Ten thousand bags would add up to well over four billion dollars today, owed by a guy making less than a hundred dollars a day. It would take him two hundred thousand years to pay the debt even if he didn't use any of his wages to feed himself or his family.

Now that's broke.

Because the servant couldn't pay, the king ordered a punishment common in the first century AD: selling the man's wife and children. A Jewish king would never have done that, but the Jewish people were under the thumb of Gentile kings at that time. So the king in Jesus's story wasn't even a God-fearing man.

The desperate servant hoped his king believed in fairness, though. He begged for fairness with a tiny drop of mercy: "Be patient with me, and I will pay back everything."

Sure you will.

The king wasn't stupid. He knew he wouldn't get his money even if he waited two hundred thousand years. Fairness, by his standards, would have been to sell the man's family. But selling them wouldn't bring him anything remotely close to four billion dollars. It wasn't worth the trouble. So instead, he took pity on the servant. He canceled the debt. He not only didn't give the man what he deserved for failing to pay a debt, *he gave him what he didn't deserve.*

In the Bible, when God doesn't give us the bad consequences we deserve, it's called mercy. When he gives us what we don't deserve, it's called grace. This king gave his servant mercy and grace.

You might think the experience of having a four-billion-dollar debt canceled would put a smile on this man's face, a spring in his step, and gratitude in his heart. Wrong. He walked out of the king's room and came face-to-face with another servant who owed him a hundred silver coins—about four thousand dollars. Enough money to feel the loss if he didn't get it back, but compared to four billion, it was nothing.

Did he smile at this man who owed him? No, he grabbed him and choked him! Even the pagan king didn't do that. And when this fellow servant said exactly what the forgiven servant had said, begging for patience and promising to pay, the forgiven guy refused. He had the man thrown into debtor's prison—where he couldn't work, so he'd never be able to earn the money to pay the debt. This wasn't a strategy for getting the four thousand. It was just revenge—a common punishment for debt in the first century.

When word of this got back to the king, he wasn't happy, and he asked the obvious question: "Shouldn't you have had mercy on your fellow servant just as I had on you?"

The answer was obvious.

JUST AS I HAD ON YOU

As obvious as the right answer is in this story, we humans find it incredibly hard not to do what the wicked servant did. The first problem we run up against is that we don't see ourselves in the shoes of a guy who owes four billion dollars.

Take a minute now and think about it. What do you owe God that you haven't paid? How much gratitude do you owe him for making you exist and for keeping you alive every day? How much worship? How much obedience because He is the King of the universe? What bad things have you done over the course of your life to people that God loves? What good things have you failed to do? When have you been wrapped up in your own concerns and not paid attention to what other people needed? To what degree have you failed to love God with your whole heart, soul, mind, and strength; and to love your neighbor?

It's hard to keep all that in your head, isn't it? Your brain gets fuzzy with a case of amnesia. It's tough to calculate years of unoffered worship, decades of ingratitude, and who knows how much disobedience and selfish lack of love. And is that really such a big deal compared to all the murderers and child abusers out there?

This is where most of us get stuck. We think our imperfect parents and annoying coworkers collectively owe us four billion dollars' worth of kindness and respect, and we're behind on maybe four thousand dollars' worth of gratitude to God. A little here, a little there, no big deal.

In fact, though, it works the other way round. We owe so much more than we are owed.

Wait, you say. I was abused by my dad, my ex, my high school teacher. My boss is on the devil's payroll. Somebody car bombed my brother in Iraq. A drunk driver killed my kid. They took things from me you can't believe. *They owe me.*

That may be true. We know people who have suffered unspeakable loss, and we don't minimize that. Maybe somebody owes you a childhood, something nobody can pay back even if they are truly sorry. Which they may not be. We won't try to put a dollar amount on what you're owed.

But here are two things:

1. You owe God more.

2. Hating that person for the rest of your life, and imagining them paying in debtor's prison forever, won't get you a dime. In fact, it will cost you and keep costing you something that money can't buy—joy. If you think about it, you know it has already cost you a lot. Unforgiveness isolates you from other people. That imaginary book where you're keeping score, and the thousand mental videos where you store memories of how others have hurt you, will do nothing but wear you down. Rewatching bad videos over and over will eat you alive.

Also, if you keep the anger inside of you, it builds and builds until you say or do something you're going to regret. The more anger you have stored up, the more it causes you to sin.

You've been harmed, and you don't want to be harmed again. That's normal, nobody does; but an unforgiving heart is not the solution. An unforgiving heart will keep you from experiencing God's mercy and grace.

Maybe you're resisting forgiveness because you have some misconceptions about what it means.

WHAT FORGIVENESS ISN'T

Forgiveness doesn't mean saying that what the person did was okay. In fact, if what they did wasn't wrong, then we don't call our response forgiveness. We call it acceptance of a perfectly okay action. Forgiveness is, by definition, a response to something a person did to us *that was wrong.*

Again, forgiveness isn't saying that what the person did was no big deal. If what they did was trivial and didn't hurt us much, then our response is called shrugging off the small stuff. Forgiveness is, by definition, a response to something a person did *that hurt us significantly.*

Forgiveness doesn't necessarily require us to let the other person close enough to do the same thing again. Sometimes, of course, it does require that. However, there are people who hurt us in such a way that we can reasonably say, "I'm not going to try to get back at you for that, but I'm not going to trust you again either, unless you show signs of significant change." That's what Miss Kay did when she and Phil were in their twenties, and Phil was drinking and not being the husband and father he needed to be. Once he saw his mistakes and was ready to make a change, she wisely wouldn't let him move back into the house and get near the boys until Phil turned his life over to the Lord and stopped the bad behaviors. She *forgave* him—she didn't nurse a grudge and she chose to want his healing rather than his punishment— before he changed. But she didn't let him close until he started to change.

The same thing happened when Alan got into trouble at seventeen. He describes that as a time when he had darkness growing inside him. He was going to church and youth group, and then sneaking off to drink and get into trouble with his girlfriend, hoping Phil wouldn't hear about it.

Phil sat him down and said, "Al, we're aware of where your life is, and it's not in a good place. If you're going to keep on with this way of living, you can't stay here in this house and impact your brothers, because I'm trying to raise them the right way."

Phil gave Alan a chance to change just as he later would with Jep, but with Alan it didn't go as well. Alan felt like he knew everything, so he picked up and left for New Orleans, Louisiana. There things spun out of control until he nearly lost his life to an angry man who wasn't happy that Alan was seeing his wife. Alan was beaten and bloodied and sitting on a street corner when he realized that if he kept on the way he was going, he wasn't going to see age nineteen.

He was like the son in another of Jesus's parables, the prodigal son in Luke 15. He was scared to go home and face Phil. He didn't expect Phil to be like the father in the Parable of the Prodigal Son, or like the king in the Parable of the Unmerciful Servant. He didn't expect to be forgiven and embraced. He'd been gone a year, and although he'd talked to his mom on the phone a few times, he hadn't spoken with his dad. So he was afraid to face Phil, but he didn't have anywhere else to go, so he went home expecting the worst.

But when he walked into the front yard, Phil went out to meet him and hugged him. Phil said he loved him and was so glad he was back. Alan expected a long list of rules and things to remind him that he'd done wrong, but what he got was unconditional forgiveness and "I'm so glad you're back." That unconditional forgiveness was what motivated Alan to finally decide to live for Christ.

So forgiving Alan didn't mean saying his behavior was okay, or that it didn't hurt. And it didn't mean letting him live in the house and influence his brothers while he was still drinking and running around with bad company. But once he came home and said, "I want to lead a different life," forgiveness meant not making him pay for the past.

It's also important to notice that Alan experienced forgiveness first and then gave his life to the Lord. Phil didn't say, "If you give your life to the Lord, then I'll forgive you." There's no guarantee that a person we forgive will weep with gratitude and commit himself to Christ. Our job is to forgive unconditionally and leave the other person's response to God. That's hard, but it's essential to our own well-being.

Notice also that forgiveness isn't an act of weakness. Phil and Miss Kay aren't weak. In fact, it takes a lot of strength to choose to cancel the debt when we're able to make the other person pay. The entire Robertson family isn't weak for loving Jep and accepting his apologies and desire to change. No, it takes strength and courage to trust someone again and give them a second chance. God certainly isn't weak and He does that for us every day.

Finally, forgiving isn't forgetting. Phil and Miss Kay remember what Alan did. Alan remembers what Jep did. When we forgive we may remember the events, but we let go of the longing to make the person pay. We quit choosing to wallow in hate and relive the wrong in our memories. This gradually frees us from having to watch the bad movie of our hurt over and over inside our heads. Scenes may flash onto our mental screens from time to time, however. And when they do, that isn't necessarily evidence that we've failed to forgive. It's evidence that we're human. But we can change that channel and not focus on the bad scenes of life.

WHAT FORGIVENESS IS

Forgiveness, by definition, is letting go of the desire to make the other person pay for an action that wronged us and caused us significant hurt. Forgiveness is saying no to revenge. It's canceling the debt. It's saying, "That action was bad, and it hurt me, and I'm canceling the debt anyway because God has canceled my debts to Him."

In the Robertson family, forgiving is a choice we make, a radical choice. We want and need God's forgiveness every day, so we must be radical in the way we forgive others who wrong us as quickly as we can.

Radical forgiveness means to forgive in such a way that others might not understand it. One reason why the world doesn't understand forgiveness is that the hurt is real. The world operates on the basis of justice (at best) and unfairness favoring the strong (a lot of the time). When a strong person cancels the debt of an unfair, wrong action that caused genuine hurt—for a lot of people in the world, that doesn't add up. They don't understand mercy and grace. But even when they don't understand, we're happy, because we've shown them something about God by the way we live. They can't see God, but they can see us doing something that comes as close to godlike as anything they will ever see.

Receiving our forgiveness—or watching us forgive someone else—can change a person's life. It can introduce them to the possibility that God forgives them. It can give them a taste of what it's like to be in a family that doesn't just put up with each other but has a real loving connection. It can make them hungry to know this forgiving God and His forgiving people. That's what happened to Phil when Miss Kay forgave him, and to Alan when Phil forgave him, and to Jep when his dad and brothers and the rest of the family forgave him. Instead of letting grudges eat away at the family's health, we choose to let forgiveness work its way from person to person in the family until it's in the family's DNA.

For twenty-two years, Alan was the pastor of an amazing church. Many people have gone to his office burdened by sins, and they've never felt judged by him because he understands what they're going through. He knows what it feels like to be guilty of serious sin, and he's experienced what it's like to be forgiven for that sin and welcomed back into the family. That's the welcome he wants to extend to others even beyond his biological family. Forgiveness for anyone who needs it.

CHANGING YOUR FOCUS

So what do you do if you want to forgive but the pain is just so bad that you feel you can't manage it? You can start by praying about it. Tell God honestly what you're feeling, and ask for help in forgiving. That's a prayer God longs to answer.

Next, try to reframe the situation in your head. God had mercy on you yesterday. And the day before that. And the day before that. He's having mercy on you right now. If you believe this deep in your bones, then the most natural thing in the world will be to treat your family and coworkers and strangers the same way.

This is why Phil forgave Alan. Not because he deserved it, but because God has forgiven Phil. We all forgive each other daily because God has forgiven us.

In our family, we make a point of regularly thinking about how we've been forgiven—by people and by God. Because God is invisible, it's easy to take His mercy for granted. It's easy to think we were forgiven a long time ago for things that weren't that bad. That's why on a regular basis we have to deliberately think about what God has done for us. Doing that changes us on the inside.

You might start by spending five minutes a day thinking about how you haven't treated God the way He deserves to be treated, how He isn't keeping score, and how in fact Jesus died on the cross so you wouldn't have to pay. Your debt is canceled. Put your mind on that, and thank Him. It will change your life.

If you really want to learn to forgive, quit focusing on what *people* have done *to* you. Put your mind on what *Jesus* has done *for* you.

If you don't believe in Jesus's death for your sins, if you haven't experienced God's grace and mercy, then forgiveness will be harder. A person who has experienced God's grace and mercy, who has let grace and mercy soak in, will become a forgiving person. But you'll find it a lot harder to forgive if you haven't received forgiveness. If you shut out God's forgiveness, you'll be insisting on getting what you deserve, and if God treats you the way you deserve, you're not going to like it.

FORGIVENESS IS A PROCESS

It's rare for someone to be able to sound like a duck that first time they blow a duck call. Like most things in life, it's a process. It's a skill you've got to learn with practice until you get the pitch and cadence right. Forgiveness is also a skill that you'll get better at with practice. Don't try to start with a really tough case, like somebody who abused you or broke your heart or killed a loved one. If you do that, you're setting yourself up for frustration and quitting.

Instead, start with forgiving friends and family for arguments and annoying habits. Start with strangers who get in the way of something you want. Build your muscles on those, and work your way up to the tough cases.

In our family, we've had years of practice and we've passed down the stories so the younger ones can understand what forgiveness is. Miss Kay passed it on to Phil, Phil passed it on to Alan and Jep, and Alan passed it on to Jep and many others. This is the best way to learn forgiveness: by seeing your family members do it over and over. By watching your parents forgive each other, by having them forgive you, by having them tell you that you need to forgive your brother for losing your fishing pole or saying mean things in a fight.

If you didn't have that kind of example growing up, you can still start now. Let Jesus be your model. God the Father can be your model of a good parent who forgives you and tells you to forgive your brothers and sisters. Jesus can show you how a good brother behaves. (Look at Luke 23:32–46 and John 8:1–11, for example. And read Jesus's parable in Luke 15:11–32.)

When you've had some practice forgiving easier things, you can start aiming at the more challenging circumstances. Just remember that forgiveness is going to be a process, not a once-and-for-all event. Don't expect yourself to get over something huge in five minutes. Start with just deciding not to dwell on thoughts of revenge and bitterness anymore. Decide (and ask the Lord's help) not to think about what you'd like to do to that person. Decide not to comfort yourself with wishing bad things on those involved. Decide never to use their sin to hurt them.

You might picture in your mind a heap of junk that represents the bad things this person has done to you and the qualities this person has that bother you. You might even stand and hold your arms like you're holding this big load of junk. Then tell the Lord you're giving all the junk to Him, and lift your arms up or turn your hands over. Drop the junk. Let it fall or float away. It's the Lord's problem, not yours anymore. Tell the Lord you're going to let Him be in charge of justice on this one. And if He wants to have mercy instead of giving this person what they deserve, you're happy with that, because you've received mercy. It's His call.

You may have to do that more than once. And don't be surprised if the bitter feelings, the anger, or the pain stay around or come back from time to time. If someone injures your knee, it can hurt for weeks. For months it'll be easy to reinjure. Your heart responds to hurt in the same way. When the pain comes back, you may have to decide all over again to forgive the person who caused the pain.

Some would say that forgiveness costs, but it usually only costs us things like pride and selfishness. Those things we don't need anyway. There are far more benefits and blessings from forgiveness than costs.

When you look at Phil or Alan or Jep today, you would never say they should have had to pay and pay for what they did. You would say, "Isn't it wonderful that they can give others the gift of mercy they've received?"

CHAPTER 3
RAVENOUS PRAYER

You won't get far building a habit of forgiveness without another habit: prayer. Our family has a ravenous hunger and an unquenchable thirst for talking and listening to God. Every episode of *Duck Dynasty*® ends in a prayer because our family believes prayer is essential to our walk with God. When people write letters and emails to the family about the show, the number-one thing they say is, "Thank you for praying to God to thank Him for the food you're fixing to eat."

We pray even more when the cameras aren't rolling than when they are. Uncle Si says he prays for God to help him relate to the fans who show up on his lawn in the middle of the night. And we depend not only on our own prayers, but also on the prayer of others. Miss Kay says,

> I have had so many people tell me that they are praying for
> our family. They realize that we have been given a huge

platform to bring God glory and reach people, and they pray for our protection, our witness, and our success in a world that Satan has owned far too long. These friends-in-prayer are praying the charge from Paul to the Colossian church—and my family feels the power of it. We will continue to speak of grace and spice it up with the style God has blessed us with—all to impact people with the gospel of Christ! Please keep the prayers going![4]

The charge that Miss Kay refers to, the one Paul gave to the Colossian church, is this:

And pray for us, too, that God may open a door for our message, so that we may proclaim the mystery of Christ, for which I am in chains. Pray that I may proclaim it clearly, as I should. Be wise in the way you act toward outsiders; make the most of every opportunity. Let your conversation be always full of grace, seasoned with salt, so that you may know how to answer everyone.

(Colossians 4:3–6)

We are so grateful that people are praying this for our family.

The Bible tells us to "pray without ceasing." That means to have a heart that is always open to God's Word and a mouth that is always willing to ask God to supply our needs. We can call on God to give us wisdom, strength, comfort, or anything else we need. God is good all the time and is always ready to listen and supply what His children need.

One day, Jesus's disciples asked Him to teach them to pray. He taught them the prayer known as the Lord's Prayer

---

4 Excerpted from *The Duck Commander Devotional* (p. 352) by permission of Howard Books.

(Luke 11:1–4). Then He told an outrageous story to make a point about the way we should approach God in prayer.

THE PARABLE OF THE FRIEND IN NEED

> Then Jesus said to them, "Suppose you have a friend, and you go to him at midnight and say, 'Friend, lend me three loaves of bread; a friend of mine on a journey has come to me, and I have no food to offer him.' And suppose the one inside answers, 'Don't bother me. The door is already locked, and my children and I are in bed. I can't get up and give you anything.' I tell you, even though he will not get up and give you the bread because of friendship, yet because of your shameless audacity he will surely get up and give you as much as you need.
>
> "So I say to you: Ask and it will be given to you; seek and you will find; knock and the door will be opened to you. For everyone who asks receives; the one who seeks finds; and to the one who knocks, the door will be opened."
>
> (Luke 11:5–10)

In the first century, hospitality was one of the most important values. If a friend came to your door at any hour of the day or night, you were expected to feed and shelter them. But there were no refrigerators or freezers in the first century, and no prepackaged foods, so people didn't keep food on hand. Even bread went quickly stale, so it was baked fresh every morning and eaten by the end of the day. In the middle of the night it was normal to have none. And there were no twenty-four-hour convenience stores either, so the host in this story was in a pickle. Honor required him to feed his guest, but the reality was that he had no food and nowhere to buy it.

He did the only possible thing: he went to his neighbor. There was a good chance that his neighbor had no food either, but it was worth a try. His neighbor tended to have more resources.

However, most people in the first century lived in one-room houses. Everybody slept in the same room, the only room. So when the host went to his neighbor's house and banged on the door, he could expect that by waking up his neighbor, he was waking up the wife and children and animals too.

It took guts to go next door and knock in the middle of the night. It took hope that his friend had bread, and it took shameless, audacious boldness not to care that his friend might be furious at him for waking up the kids.

The friend did what most people would do. He said, "Don't bother me."

Now the host had a choice. Would he take no for an answer? Or would he keep pounding on the door, begging for bread?

What would you do? Would you worry about being a burden to your neighbor? Would you be afraid of rejection, fearing more words like "Don't bother me"? Jesus and the people hearing His parable knew that the normal thing—the considerate, respectful thing—to do would be to back off. Hammering on your neighbor's door at midnight is an extreme behavior. But in this outrageous story, because there was a hungry guest needing food, shameless audacity was called for.

The Greek word translated "shameless audacity" here is *anaideian*. It is often rendered as "boldness," but no English word quite captures its sense of nerve and complete indifference to embarrassment or rejection. Picture Uncle Si pounding on that door all night if he has to, not caring if the whole town hears him.

Jesus made the story even more shocking by saying that the neighbor wasn't even a generous enough person to get out of bed and give the bread because of friendship. It was solely the obnoxious persistence of the host that got action.

Jesus was challenging His disciples to think about how they viewed God. Did they see God as being like this neighbor, sleepy and indifferent to friends? Even if God is like that, Jesus was saying, you should still bang on His door. And you should bang away even more, because God has all the bread in the universe and actually does care about His friends! If shameless audacity works with self-centered people like this neighbor, it works even better with God.

WHO IS GOD?

How do you view God? Because He made the universe and His thoughts are farther above yours than your thoughts are above those of termites, maybe you feel you should get near God only when you're desperate. Or if you had parents who left you to fend for yourself, maybe you see God that way: He's out there somewhere, but for practical purposes you're on your own. If you had harsh parents, maybe you see God as harsh. These are a few of the common distorted views people have of God.

On the other hand, maybe you feel like nobody in this world is above you, and you have the right to march into the White House if you feel like it and tell the president what to do. Maybe you carry that same attitude into prayer, telling God what He'd better do and getting mad if He doesn't jump to it.

Shameless audacity isn't disrespect. Our family doesn't go to God demanding that He do things. But we don't hesitate to go to God asking Him to do things, because He's said He wants to hear from us, because we know He's generous, and because it's midnight and He's the only one in town with bread.

Do you feel like God is ignoring your cries for bread? He's not ignoring you. He's just waiting so you'll learn to pray ravenously, shamelessly, with total humility and dependence. He won't necessarily give you everything you want, but He will give you what you need.

As with faith, so with prayer: feelings aren't a good guide. You may not feel God's presence when you pray, but He's there.

We think it's important for a family to develop a habit of praying together about things that affect the whole family. This is one of the ways the younger generation learns how to pray. Here's how my (Korie's) son John Luke talks about the way our family prepares for events where we're going to speak in public:

> When we are asked to speak as a group, everyone will take a turn praying for the event and the words we say. We don't assign prayer topics; everyone prays for whatever they have on their hearts.

If you start doing this with kids when they're small, they grow up feeling that it's normal. It doesn't matter if your words sound good. What matters is that you talk with God ravenously in front of your kids.

ASK, SEEK, KNOCK

Jesus told His parable to get a response, and then He spelled out the response He wanted: "Ask and it will be given to you; seek and you will find; knock and the door will be opened to you." Ask, seek, knock—these verbs get bolder and bolder. To ask is to request something humbly and maybe politely, like a child's first request for a cookie. To seek is braver— this is an active pursuit. The men in our family don't just ask for catfish or frogs or ducks. They go looking for them. They get up in the darkest, coldest time before dawn. They wade in freezing water. They wait. And wait. They don't quit. You can't seek ducks in your cozy living room.

Knocking takes us back to the parable. This isn't just a few shy taps on a door. This is pounding until God comes and opens it. Seeking and knocking for big things like the salvation of your family may take a lifetime. Don't quit.

God promises He won't reject ravenous prayer. It *will* be given to you. You *will* find. The door *will* be opened. Not if you tap once and put your feet up where you're comfortable, though. God will answer if you keep asking, keep wading out into the cold water to seek, keep hammering on that door.

PHIL IN MEMPHIS

Here's a story about prayer that makes me (Korie) want to laugh because it says so much about how God works in Phil's life. Phil was once driving down the road, and the phone in his truck rang. The woman on the phone said, "Mr. Robertson, I tried to reach you at your workplace, but they said you were on a trip. They gave me the number to your truck, and I'm calling you up to ask you to do a big favor for me."

"What's that, ma'am?" Phil said.

"My son has come down with a rare form of leukemia," she said. "He's in the hospital and they give him like a 10 percent chance to live. And I'm asking you, is it possible in your travels to go by that hospital and pray for him?"

"Well, where is the hospital?" Phil asked.

She said it was St. Jude's in Memphis, Tennessee. Phil saw a road sign that said, "Memphis—2 Miles." Phil was astounded because he was on the road hundreds of miles from home and he could hardly remember where all he had been.

"Your son's in Memphis?" he said. "Well, ma'am, I'm actually two miles out of Memphis. I'm coming from Arkansas, going toward the Mississippi River bridge."

"Well, that's great," she said, "because right on the other side of the bridge when you cross the Mississippi River is St. Jude's Hospital."

"I am now coming up on the bridge," he said. "I will go in and pray for your son."

He looked at Miss Kay next to him in the truck and said, "What are the odds of someone calling and asking me to pray for their son in a hospital in Memphis, Tennessee and I'm just coming up on Memphis, Tennessee?"

Miss Kay said, "I think the Almighty's got a hand in that."

They went into the hospital and found the young fellow lying on his back with tubes in his nose and his head shaved.

"How are you doing, Mr. Robertson?" the young man said.

"Well, son," Phil said, "I'm doing a lot better than you are. But I think God is going to deliver you from this terrible illness, and we're going to ask Him to do that. What I want you to understand is when you get on your feet you have a free duck hunt. Get your buddy and I'll take both of you duck hunting when you get on your feet and get your strength back. That'll give you something to look forward to."

Phil prayed that God would deliver him from his debilitating disease, and he left.

Several months went by, and Phil was back in Memphis at the Ducks Unlimited Outdoor Festival. A young man walked up to him. He had his hair now.

"Mr. Robertson, do you remember me?" he asked.

"Son," Phil said, "I don't think I remember you. Who are you?"

"I was the fellow you prayed for in the hospital. The sickness all went away."

"And now you're calling me on that duck hunt," Phil said.

"Yes, sir. You said you'd carry me."

"You get your buddy," Phil said. "You call me in October, closer to duck season, and I'll take you both duck hunting. I'm glad to see that you're alive and well."

"Thank you, Mr. Robertson, for praying for me," the young man said.

In the fall he came down with his buddy, they went duck hunting, and the mallard ducks just poured down into the duck hole in front of them. They had a great duck hunt, full limits.

Jase was with Phil, and he said later, "You know what? I not only think that God raised him up off his sick bed, but I've never seen that many ducks come down in that hole, have you?"

"No," Phil said, "I think God sent them too."

God is good. One prayer, one young man, one day in history. He's still alive on the earth. His momma is thrilled, and so are we. An atheist would say it was luck. It might have been luck, but Phil attributes it to the Creator of the cosmos. God can do anything.

HOW TO PRAY: THE PSALMS

Some people feel like they don't know what to say in prayer. The first answer to that is, "Say whatever is on your mind. Just say it." If you know how to talk, you know how to pray. You can talk to God in plain English.

If you want more help, the Bible is full of examples of prayers that can give you a vocabulary of prayer. The book of Psalms, for instance, contains the lyrics of 150 songs that can be thought of as sung prayers. Try reading one of those a day and seeing what you can learn from these songwriters who were ravenous in what they said to God.

Look at how David bangs on God's door in Psalm 5:

> Listen to my words, LORD,
> consider my lament.
> Hear my cry for help,
>   my King and my God,
> for to you I pray.
> In the morning, LORD, you hear my voice;
>   in the morning I lay my requests before you
>   and wait expectantly.
> For you are not a God who is pleased with wickedness;
>   with you, evil people are not welcome.
> The arrogant cannot stand
>   in your presence.

You hate all who do wrong;
    you destroy those who tell lies.
The bloodthirsty and deceitful
    you, LORD, detest.
But I, by your great love,
    can come into your house;
in reverence I bow down
toward your holy temple.
Lead me, LORD, in your righteousness
    because of my enemies —
    make your way straight before me.
Not a word from their mouth can be trusted;
    their heart is filled with malice.
Their throat is an open grave;
    with their tongues they tell lies.
Declare them guilty, O God!
    Let their intrigues be their downfall.
Banish them for their many sins,
    for they have rebelled against you.
But let all who take refuge in you be glad;
    let them ever sing for joy.
Spread your protection over them,
    that those who love your name may rejoice in you.
Surely, LORD, you bless the righteous;
    you surround them with your favor as with a shield.

David starts by crying out, "Listen! Hear!" He reminds himself and God that God does listen. He says he waits in expectation for God to do something. He talks about God's character, how God is the kind of person who cares about the very thing David is praying for. He expresses confidence in God. He also vents his emotions about the people who are trying to undermine him: "Their throat is an open grave; /

with their tongues they tell lies. / ... Let their intrigues be their downfall. Banish them for their many sins."

David isn't wringing his hands and mumbling, "Lord, I just really would like you to just bless me ... " He's shouting, "Listen to me, Lord! Let me tell You what I really think about these people! I'm not going to mince my words with You. Protect me so I can rejoice in You. That's the kind of God You are." David doesn't fake it with God. He's shameless and audacious and ravenous.

HOW TO PRAY: THE LORD'S PRAYER

The best-known prayer in the Bible is called the Lord's Prayer because Jesus gave it to His disciples (Matthew 6:9–13; Luke 11:2–4). Luke's version is the briefer one, just an outline of issues to address in prayer:

> "Father,
> hallowed be your name,
> your kingdom come.
> Give us each day our daily bread.
> Forgive us our sins,
>   for we also forgive everyone who sins against us.
> And lead us not into temptation."

Jesus teaches us to approach God as a trusting child goes to a caring father. That trust goes with respect—God's name (His identity and character) should be "hallowed" or treated as holy. We're not giving orders to someone we can vote out of office if he doesn't do our will. We're asking things of Someone who made us and can unmake us.

Then before we ask anything for ourselves, we pray for God's agenda. We ask that God's kingdom—the realm where what He wants done is done without resistance—will be fully present on earth. We live in a fallen and broken world, but one day God will put everything right and reign as King here as He does throughout the heavens. We pray our here-and-now requests in light of that promised eternity.

We depend on God for our basic needs: daily bread. There was a time in the life of the Robertson family when some days there was not much on the table but bread and fried bologna. God doesn't promise us a feast every day. But He does provide what we need to survive, and that's enough to be grateful for.

Forgiveness is another theme of this prayer. We ask for forgiveness and we give forgiveness to everyone who has sinned against us.

Finally, we pray for protection from temptation. "Lead us not into temptation" means "Keep us from giving in to temptation." We depend on God not just for food and forgiveness, but for the power to stay away from sin. We are so prone to sin. Obedience is hard. We need to ask God to empower us to obey Him.

Notice that we're not asking to be rich and famous. We're asking to have enough to live on, to be forgiven, to be protected from our attraction to sin, to see God on the throne of the universe, to see God's name treated as holy.

WHAT'S ON YOUR HEART?

What is on your heart to ask God to do? Do you need Him to provide your daily bread? Do you need protection from temptation and evil? Maybe you want to forgive someone and you need God's help to let go of the bitterness. Maybe you want to have strong faith that takes action based on unshakable trust in God's goodness. Why not stop right now and tell God what's on your heart? Be shameless, audacious, radical.

We usually end our prayers with the word *amen*. It's from a Hebrew adverb that means "so be it." We (Korie and Chrys) ask God to grant your ravenous prayer in the mighty name of His Son, Jesus. Amen!

CHAPTER 4

REAL OBEDIENCE

I (Korie) have described how when Alan was a teenager, he left his family and tried to live life without his parents or God. He disobeyed Phil and Miss Kay, and when they tried to get him to turn his life around, he moved far away.

Some might think that's the worst kind of son to have. But it's not. Alan eventually realized that Miss Kay and Phil wanted the best for him. He went home and left the bad life behind. Since that time, Alan has honored his parents and followed God.

Compare that to a son who never drinks, never uses drugs, and goes to church every Sunday, but is selfish, critical, and downright cruel to his wife and children behind closed doors. A son who does those things and never changes course because he never figures out that he needs to. That's the worst kind of son to have: one who says yes to God on the surface but keeps on saying no, no, no to God by the way he lives. It's terribly hard on a parent when a son goes off and does wrong the way Alan did, but it's hard in another way when a son says all the right things but doesn't walk the talk.

That's exactly what Jesus tells us in a parable about two sons.

THE PARABLE OF THE TWO SONS

Here's what Jesus said:

> "What do you think? There was a man who had two sons. He went to the first and said, 'Son, go and work today in the vineyard.'
>
> "'I will not,' he answered, but later he changed his mind and went.
>
> "Then the father went to the other son and said the same thing. He answered, 'I will, sir,' but he did not go.
>
> "Which of the two did what his father wanted?"
>
> "The first," they answered.
>
> Jesus said to them, "Truly I tell you, the tax collectors and the prostitutes are entering the kingdom of God ahead of you. For John came to you to show you the way of righteousness, and you did not believe him, but the tax collectors and the prostitutes did. And even after you saw this, you did not repent and believe him."
>
> (Matthew 21:28–32)

Like the rest of the parables, this story came from everyday life in the world around Jesus. Grapes were one of the main crops in that part of the world, and everybody had at least seen a vineyard. Many had worked in one.

Jesus told this story to the religious leaders who opposed Him. These leaders were at the top of the social ladder, and the tax collectors and prostitutes were at the bottom. Tax collectors were hated because they served the Roman regime that had invaded the Jewish homeland. A chief tax collector agreed to collect a certain sum of money in an area, and anything he could extort from the people above that sum was his to keep. Chief tax collectors employed gangs of roughnecks who did the dirty work of collection. Neither the chiefs nor their gangs were welcome in decent society, but they made good money and didn't care that they couldn't enter a house of worship.

The "John" mentioned in this story was the prophet John the Baptist, a cousin of Jesus. He had a massive preaching and baptizing ministry in the years leading up to Jesus's public ministry. Crowds went out to the Jordan River to be baptized in the water by John and his followers as a sign of turning away from sin. Among them were tax collectors. Matthew, one of Jesus's closest followers, was a former tax collector (Matthew 9:9–13). Tax collectors were practically criminals, yet there they were—responding obediently to what John and Jesus taught them to do—while the religious leaders rejected both John and Jesus.

John taught "the way of righteousness"—how someone who is in right relationship with God lives. His guidance to people in general and to tax collectors was simple:

> "What should we do then?" the crowd asked.
>
> John answered, "Anyone who has two shirts should share with the one who has none, and anyone who has food should do the same."
>
> Even tax collectors came to be baptized. "Teacher," they asked, "what should we do?"
>
> "Don't collect any more than you are required to," he told them.
>
> (Luke 3:10–13)

Real obedience for everybody involved generosity to share even the most basic things like food and clothing. And obedience for tax collectors started when they stopped extorting more money from the people than the Romans demanded.

Jesus's story contrasts two kinds of people: the type of religious person who knows and says all the right things about God but doesn't do the right things; and the person who may have run away from God for a long time but now has turned around and is obeying Him. God would rather have someone who says no and then changes his mind than someone who keeps saying yes but is all talk and no action.

WHY DID THE SECOND SON SAY YES?

Our word *obey* comes from the Latin *obedire, oboedire*, which means to be subject, serve, or pay attention to. One of the Greek words for "obey" means to be under someone's authority; another means to trust. Real obedience involves trusting and paying attention to someone. It involves serving someone, being subject to their authority. True Christian obedience is not about following a rule for no reason; it's about loving someone so much that you want to follow the rules.

Jesus intended His hearers to think about His stories, to chew on them over time. One useful question to chew on is, "Why did the second son say yes and then not follow through?" Jesus didn't say why, but the story invites us to think about the possibilities. This can help us understand ourselves when we find ourselves saying yes but not following through. Why do we do it? There are a range of reasons that need to be handled differently.

First, maybe the son said yes while fully knowing he

had no intention of obeying. He was deliberately trying to deceive his father. His pride or selfishness made him not want to obey, but possibly he didn't want the conflict and consequences that would come from open refusal. So he pretended more loyalty than he had. He was a simple hypocrite.

On the other hand, maybe when he said yes, he didn't know he intended to disobey. He was deceiving himself about his level of trust and love for his father. He didn't know how selfish he really was. He had never admitted to himself that his life revolved around himself and what he wanted. A person like this needs to become aware of his self-deceit as well as dealing with his hypocrisy.

Another possibility is that maybe when he said yes, he fully intended to obey, but something got in the way. He needs to identify that something. Did he forget because he was too busy? If so, he needs to address his priorities, because saying yes to everything means some things will get an "accidental" no. He's not superhuman.

Did he say yes because he was a people pleaser? If so, he needs to decide who he will please and whose displeasure he will face head on. He needs to come to love his father so much that the desire to please him will flow from love.

Maybe he said yes because he knew he was supposed to, but something else came along and tempted him. A person like this needs to get control of his desires instead of letting them control him.

Or did he say yes without counting the cost, and when the cost confronted him, his loyalty to his father proved to be shallow? If so, he needs to develop the habit of facing the costs of obedience, and he needs to do some deliberate thinking about how much his father's authority really means to him.

You can see that getting over a habit of disobedience often requires facing whatever is driving the disobedience. If you want to obey but don't follow through, ask yourself, "Who or what am I paying attention to, trusting, serving, and being subject to ahead of God?" It could be yourself or someone else. It could be some desire, such as safety, comfort, status, fun, lust, greed, or what-will-people-think. Real obedience comes from the heart, so these heart issues need to be our focus. If we focus simply on the outward behavior, we're unlikely to be deeply obedient over time. We're more likely to be hypocrites, saying yes but not following through.

WHY OBEY?

There are some very good reasons for obeying God. One is that *when we obey God, He often amazes us by the good things He can do through us.* For instance, back when Uncle Si was in the military, God said to him at one point, "You're going back to Germany."

"No, I'm not," Si said. "I'm sick of it. This time I ain't going." Si got with his superiors and said, "Hey, I've been over there four or five times. Some two years, some three."

"Yup, you're off orders," his superiors finally said. "You're not going."

Then the next thing he knew, his commanding officer said, "You and your family are catching a plane next week to Germany. Here's your orders. Get ready to go."

Si wasn't happy about it, but he and his wife and daughter got on the plane. When they landed in Frankfurt, Germany,

Si expected somebody from his unit would be there to pick him up. He waited a couple of hours, and finally he phoned the base.

"No, you're not here," they said.

"Oh yes, we're here," Si said. "Send somebody to pick us up."

"You've got no orders," they said.

Something was fouled up. But in the meantime, Si and his family went to base and found a congregation to worship with. A young couple there had three kids that needed a grandfather and grandmother. Si realized that God had been saying, "Yes, you're going, because I need you there to be a grandfather to this family and mentor them and help take care of them." So that's what Uncle Si and Aunt Christine did for three years.

You never know where God is going to put you. He's got something for you to do there, but you won't find out what it is unless you're doing what He says. If God can turn the Robertson family into TV stars, He can do anything. He may not make you a star, but He will put you to work for His glory if you let Him.

Another reason to obey is that if we don't, the consequences can be bad. God told Jonah to preach to the people of Nineveh in what is now Iraq. Jonah hated those people because they were the enemies of Israel and had done about the worst things you can do in war to civilians. Even in a time when most armies committed what we would call war crimes, and everybody expected it, the Ninevites were legendary for committing atrocities that would turn your stomach. So Jonah caught the first boat to the other end of the known world: Tarshish in what is now Spain. But he never got there, because God sent a storm that nearly sank his ship. The sailors had to throw him overboard to save themselves, and Jonah was swallowed by a whale.

And then there was Moses, who was a hero of obedience to God. Moses obediently confronted Pharaoh and led the Israelites out of slavery in Egypt. He obediently led them to Mount Sinai and was given the Law for them to live by. He obediently led them through the desert to the Promised Land. But there was one day when Moses was disobedient, and it cost him. He and the people were traveling through the desert, and the people complained that they needed water. God told Moses to speak to a rock and water would pour out. But Moses was tired and frustrated, so he hit the rock with his staff and shouted angrily at the people. Water gushed from the rock, but God said, "Because you did not trust in me enough to honor me as holy in the sight of the Israelites, you will not bring this community into the land I give them" (Numbers 20:12). Moses led the people up to the edge of the Promised Land, but he died there, and Joshua led the people into the land.

Even for Moses, there was a cost for disobedience.

Sometimes we know when we pay a price for disobedience, but sometimes we're blind to the price. We don't realize that weak or broken relationships could have been strong and could have made our lives richer if we had approached them the way God wanted us to. We don't see the connection between disobedience and our troubles with money. Suffering happens even to the most obedient believer, but sometimes it can be lessened, handled better, or avoided if we're living the way God tells us to live in the Bible.

That leads to the third reason to obey, which is that *obedience is actually good for us.* Obedience doesn't earn God's love. It doesn't earn our right standing before God—only Jesus's sacrifice does that. But as Uncle Si said once, "God made the law to *protect* people, not *enslave* them ... it is for our *good.* Obeying it makes life and relationship sweeter."[5] When we rightly understand God's instructions and don't burden ourselves with expectations of perfect performance, we find out that aiming at obedience makes life better, not worse.

In Psalm 128 we read:

> Blessed are all who fear the LORD,
>   who walk in obedience to him.
> You will eat the fruit of your labor;
>   blessings and prosperity will be yours.
> Your wife will be like a fruitful vine
>   within your house;
> your children will be like olive shoots
>   around your table.
> Yes, this will be the blessing
>   for the man who fears the LORD.
>
>   (Psalm 128:1–4)

When Phil finally decided to follow Jesus in his twenties, the pastor gave him two things to try: Love God and love your neighbor.

"Try to be good," he said.

Phil said, "I've never tried that before."

"Just try," the man said.

The difficulty was this: Phil was making ends meet as a

---

5   Excerpted from *The Duck Commander Devotional* (p. 281) by permission of Howard Books.

commercial fisherman at that time, and there were men he calls "river rats" who would actually steal the fish from his nets before he could take them to market. He was reading in Romans 12, "do not repay anyone evil for evil," but Phil had a family to feed. Usually when he came upon men stealing his fish, he'd raise his shotgun and say, "The next person who moves, dies."

"They're stealing my fish, Lord," Phil said in prayer.

But the Bible said, "If they're hungry, feed them" and "Do not return evil for evil."

"You want me to do what?" Phil said.

One day Phil was watching through the bushes as two men pulled up in a boat next to Phil's float, where his net was submerged in the river. He said to himself that he was going to be good to these men, but he was carrying his shotgun just in case they weren't good to him.

He roared up on them just as they were pulling his net up into their boat.

"What were you boys doing with that net?" he said.

"Is that what that was?" they said.

"Yeah. That's a hook net. It belongs to me. Now here's the good news. I'm going to raise the net, and whatever fish are in there, I'm going to give them to you."

When he said that, they looked at each other with eyes wide. He gave them the fish, and when they rode away in their boat they were looking back at him like he was a crazy man. But after that, up and down the river they quit stealing his fish.

God was right all along about doing good to those who do evil.

Even though we are saved by grace, obedience still

matters. Some people make the mistake of thinking that trusting in God's grace means taking no action themselves. That's a misunderstanding of faith and grace. A lady once told Si she needed a job. Si said, "Hey, have you put any résumés in?"

She said, "No, God will take care of it."

Si said, "No, He won't, not if you don't do your part. You've got to respond to what He has for you to do." God is longing to do His part, but He will never do our part for us. Our part is obedience.

A fourth reason to obey is simply that *God deserves it*. The Father loved you enough to create you, and then sent His Son to die for you. His Son loved you enough to willingly take your place on the cross. The Father loves you enough to send the Holy Spirit to dwell in you if you believe in Christ.

During His earthly ministry, Jesus and His disciples once had to cross the Sea of Galilee in a boat. A storm came up, and waves crashed over the boat. Jesus was asleep, but His disciples woke Him and said, "Lord, save us! We're going to drown." Jesus rebuked the wind and waves, and the sea became calm. His amazed disciples said, "What kind of man is this? Even the winds and the waves obey him!" (Matthew 8:23–27).

Even the wind and waves obey Jesus, because He made them. Shouldn't you also obey Him, because He made you?

FUELED BY LOVE

Angrily going through the motions of obedience will drain the life out of you in the long run. You don't have to feel loving all the time, but if you obey grudgingly, resentfully, it will show. Real obedience is fueled by the experience of being loved. As the apostle John said, "We love because he first loved us" (1 John 4:19). Obedience fueled by the experience of being loved doesn't run out of gas.

"But wait," someone might say, "John says 'we love' not 'we obey.'" Jesus, though, said obeying God is the same as loving God and others:

> "As the Father has loved me, so have I loved you. Now remain in my love. If you keep my commands, you will remain in my love, just as I have kept my Father's commands and remain in his love.... My command is this: Love each other as I have loved you. Greater love has no one than this: to lay down one's life for one's friends. You are my friends if you do what I command.... This is my command: Love each other."
>
> (John 15:9–10, 12–14, 17)

John echoes this. "And this is love: that we walk in obedience to his commands. As you have heard from the beginning, his command is that you walk in love" (2 John 1:6).

God deserves to be loved, respected, obeyed. He created us. He died for us. He continues to sustain us with every breath. Love and respect for God are settled states of the heart, not flighty emotions. We may not always feel respectful, we may feel angry or afraid at times, but at our core we either respect Him or we don't.

Of course, nobody is perfectly obedient to God. We all fall short and rely on God's forgiveness. What God longs to see in you is not perfect performance but a daily decision to be a certain kind of child to your heavenly Father. Not the kind who says, "No way!" Not the kind who says yes but then doesn't follow through. But the kind who consistently does what your Maker asks of you, because you love and trust Him.

CHAPTER 5

ROWDY KINDNESS

When Willie was eighteen, he started seminary and had no money. He was working with the youth group at the church and he really loved doing that, but he was struggling financially. When some wealthier members at church heard about this, they gave him money to help him along.

The person whose kindness Willie most remembers, though, was not one of the wealthy people. It was a sweet little lady named Miss Willa. She had a great laugh and Willie loved being around her. Miss Willa came up to Willie one day in the church lobby and said, "Willie Jess, I'm going to give you something because I know you need a little extra help." She gave Willie a ten dollar bill. Willie took the money from Miss Willa because he was broke enough to need ten dollars. He put it in his pocket and said, "Thank you so much, Miss Willa."

That ten dollars meant so much to Willie, even more

than all the gifts from the wealthier people, because it really cost Miss Willa something. Willie knew she was investing in him. She loved Willie and even though it wasn't much, it was the perfect amount to let Willie know she believed in him. Her investment in him helped Willie get through seminary and college and on to where he is now. Willie has never forgotten what Miss Willa did.

When Mom and I talked about how we wanted to name this chapter, we came up with the word *rowdy* because it really means to be *loud* about being kind. Miss Willa had some rowdy kindness. She was not afraid to offer Willie a small amount of money because she knew it was a big investment in him. Most of the time, other people might not appreciate us being rowdy, but when it comes to being kind to others, it's great to be out loud on purpose. Being rowdy about kindness means to choose to treat everyone you meet with a kind and respectful spirit. Rowdy kindness is the opposite of the meanness and bullying that you can see all over the Internet, in schools, and in many families. Rowdy kindness is an important value in our family because it pulls people together instead of pushing them apart.

To treat others kindly and respectfully, we have to look at them as God sees them. We have to forget about everything except God's desire that we are kind, no matter what. That's hard to do sometimes.

Phil was once on another TV show where a man got mad at him and at the Robertson family, calling him names. All Phil said was, "I love him anyway."

This is contrary to the way the world works. It reminds us of the time Jesus found Himself in a conversation with a lawyer. To show just how rowdy He expects our kindness to be, Jesus told one of His most shocking stories.

THE PARABLE OF THE GOOD SAMARITAN

On one occasion an expert in the law stood up to test Jesus. "Teacher," he asked, "what must I do to inherit eternal life?"

"What is written in the Law?" he replied. "How do you read it?"

He answered, "'Love the Lord your God with all your heart and with all your soul and with all your strength and with all your mind'; and, 'Love your neighbor as yourself.'"

"You have answered correctly," Jesus replied. "Do this and you will live."

But he wanted to justify himself, so he asked Jesus, "And who is my neighbor?"

In reply Jesus said: "A man was going down from Jerusalem to Jericho, when he was attacked by robbers. They stripped him of his clothes, beat him and went away, leaving him half dead. A priest happened to be going down the same road, and when he saw the man, he passed by on the other side. So too, a Levite, when he came to the place and saw him, passed by on the other side. But a Samaritan, as he traveled, came where the man was; and when he saw him, he took pity on him. He went to him and bandaged his wounds, pouring on oil and wine. Then he put the man on his own donkey, brought him to an inn and took care of him. The next day he took out two denarii and gave them to the innkeeper. 'Look after him,' he said, 'and when I return, I will reimburse you for any extra expense you may have.'

"Which of these three do you think was a neighbor to the man who fell into the hands of robbers?"

The expert in the law replied, "The one who had mercy on him."

Jesus told him, "Go and do likewise."

(Luke 10:25–37)

LOOKING FOR A LOOPHOLE

This whole conversation was designed as a test of Jesus, but it turned out to be a test of the expert in the Jewish Law. The man correctly identified the Old Testament's main teaching about how to live: Love God with your whole being, and deal with people in light of that love. But having given the right answer, the legal expert was uncomfortable with it. Loving your neighbor with the same attention and commitment you give to looking after yourself is a tall order. So he aimed for a loophole: who counts as a *neighbor*? Surely that meant only devout members of his own ethnic group, not outsiders. Surely not sinners.

Jesus replied by telling a story that the legal expert almost certainly found offensive. A Jewish man, he said, was on the road from Jerusalem to Jericho. That road—as everybody at the time knew—was eighteen miles long and descended about 3,500 feet. After about two miles there was a village named Bethany; then the road became very rough with many rocky caves where bandits hid. This area was called the "bloody way." It was too dangerous for a man to travel alone—not unlike some of the worst parts of our inner cities or notorious roads in modern Afghanistan.

Not surprisingly, robbers attacked the traveler and left him for dead. Sometime later, two of the most admired members of society passed by. The priest and the Levite were both religious professionals. For reasons Jesus didn't give, they decided not to get involved. Their reasons may have been understandable—touching a corpse would have made them unclean for temple work for a period of time, or the injured man could have been a decoy in an ambush—but the reasons aren't the point. These men decided not to act with rowdy kindness. That role was left to a Samaritan.

Jesus's choice of a Samaritan doesn't hit us the way it would have hit His original audience. In Jewish eyes, Samaritans were ethnically mixed members of a quasi-Jewish cult. They were descended from Jews intermarried with pagans. People like the legal expert despised them so much that the word *Samaritan* wouldn't have been a polite enough word to use on network TV. Think of the worst racial stereotype you can imagine. Just mentioning those people would have raised the hairs on the back of the legal expert's neck. And the idea of a *good* Samaritan would have made about as much sense to him as a good Nazi. But this Samaritan treated the injured man as a neighbor.

The Samaritan "took pity" on him. The Greek word *splagchnizomai* means "to be moved as to one's innards." A person's abdominal organs represented the warm, tender emotions you get when you do something kind for or "take pity" on someone else.

There were no hospitals, so the Samaritan gave the injured man first aid and took him to an inn. He gave the innkeeper two denarii—two days' wages, enough for two weeks in an inn—and promised to pay whatever else it cost to care for the man.

That's rowdy kindness. The legal expert had asked, "Who is my neighbor?" Jesus asked, "Who acted as a neighbor?" In his reply, the legal expert couldn't even bring himself to say the word *Samaritan*.

Jesus calls us to be a neighbor like that to anybody in need. This is what Miss Willa did, giving a precious ten dollars to

Willie. This is what a bus driver did recently. There was a woman about to jump off a bridge, and people were walking by and doing nothing. But a bus driver stopped a bus full of people, got out, talked the woman down, grabbed her, and pulled her back over the ledge. Who knows what the bus riders were thinking when their driver stopped the bus and got out, but this was a time when kindness to a stranger was more important than getting someplace on schedule.

After Phil started to follow Christ, he and Miss Kay knew the right decision was to treat everyone they met with kindness. They'd see somebody on the side of the road and say, "Y'all need something to eat?" They'd pick the people up in their truck, take them down to the house by the river, feed them, let them stay a couple of days, even give them a little money. Phil and Miss Kay didn't have a lot of money at that time, but they wanted to share Jesus with people and they did it through rowdy kindness.

That's how Jesus teaches us to be. When we see someone in need, we stop and help them, no matter what. It may not be cool. We may be in a hurry. We may not want to get involved. But we give kindness anyway.

WHY BE KIND?

What you do doesn't earn God's approval, but it matters for a lot of reasons.

First, *it's a response to God's kindness to you.* As the apostle John said,

> This is how God showed his love among us: He sent his one and only Son into the world that we might live through him. This is love: not that we loved God, but that he loved

us and sent his Son as an atoning sacrifice for our sins. Dear friends, since God so loved us, we also ought to love one another. No one has ever seen God; but if we love one another, God lives in us and his love is made complete in us.

(1 John 4:9–12)

"Since God so loved us, we also ought to love one another." It's that simple. We treat others as we've been treated.

Or as the apostle Paul said, "Therefore, as God's chosen people, holy and dearly loved, clothe yourselves with compassion, kindness, humility, gentleness and patience" (Colossians 3:12). If we know ourselves to be chosen by God, dearly loved, and set apart to be His holy people, then compassion and kindness ought to flow from us to others.

Second, *kindness is how you build a healthy family or workplace.* There's a practical side to kindness: it's the glue that holds together relationships like the ones you see in our family. Those relationships don't hold solid under stress by magic. They hold because we cultivate habits of kindness and respect.

Even though the guys seem to get on each other's nerves on the *Duck Dynasty*® show to be funny, there's a lot of kindness and warmth at the Duck Commander warehouse, people doing things for others. If you're going to push a company to grow as big as Duck Commander has gotten, there has to be kindness. You can't just whip them to work harder. You say, "I can help you out; you can help me out."

Third, *kindness demonstrates to people who don't believe in God that God's people are different.* Jesus told His followers, "A new command I give you: Love one another. As I have loved you, so you must love one another. By this everyone will know that you are my disciples, if you love one another" (John

13:34–35). People tell our family that one of the main things that draws them to watch our show and listen to us is the way we treat each other. Outsiders aren't interested in hearing about Christ from unkind Christians. They expect Christians to behave better than the average person, and when we don't, they notice. If we, believers and followers of Jesus, don't act any differently than those who don't know Jesus, how can we impact the world? The world *has* to see something different in us.

Now that you have some reasons to be kind, what can you do if kindness doesn't come naturally?

GROWING IN KINDNESS

God can shape you to be kind, even if you're not a very kind person.

Willie remembers that when he was growing up, Phil made a real transformation in his life. He went from being a terrible guy to the kind man we know today. When Willie was young, Phil said things that weren't kind, and Willie always pushed himself with the thought, "You know what, I'm not going to be like that." He saw the sin in Phil's life, and Willie went the other way and said, "Man, I'm going to be kind and speak kindly from a good heart." And the remarkable thing is that Phil made that same transformation. If he can do it with God's help, so can you.

The first thing you can do is *pray for God's help*. This is another prayer that God loves to answer. Start praying this, and don't give up.

Next, *notice the audio playing in your head*. If you're focused on the raw deal you've gotten in life and how nobody else is kind to you so you have to look out for yourself, you're going to find it hard to be rowdy in kindness for very long. It won't be coming from your heart, the core of you. Listen in on your inner monologue. Are you saying to yourself, "Everybody out there is selfish. Nobody has ever looked out for me, so I have to look out for myself. It's my life, and I get to live it my way. I'm in a hurry. I don't have time to stop for everybody with a sob story. I am busy busy busy. Too much is expected of me already ..."? If that's the voice in your head, you'll need to be honest with yourself about it. Then start telling yourself something different: "God has been unbelievably kind to me. Look at this and this that he's done for me. And look at how that person was kind to that other person. That's how I want to be. Sometimes being kind is more important than being efficient ..."

Third, try to *see people the way Jesus sees them*. They're not just bodies in your way. They're not just tools for fulfilling your needs. They're living, precious individuals—each one made by God to reflect something of Him in the world. They have feelings the way you do. If they were the only person on earth, and you weren't here, Jesus would still have died for them. If you have trouble caring about people, ask God to help you see them the way Jesus does, and then make the effort to really look at them.

Fourth, *look around you for needs*. This will require you to tune out some other things. You may need to turn off the music you like to play or put away your phone for periods of time. Constant connection to electronic devices can get in the way of noticing people. Make the person you're with a priority over those who are texting you. Notice other people in the grocery store aisle; how can you be kind to them? Pay attention to people who look lost or homeless or upset. This is very difficult in today's world because of our electronics, but it's not impossible. Just do it!

If you tend to get overwhelmed by huge needs that need a big organization and lots of money, try looking locally for ways individual people need help. Start with friends and family, and spread out from there. Practice *noticing*. Again, we are challenged today because our noticing eyes and ears are busy with our phones or other electronic things. But decide that you want to notice others and then practice doing kind things in small ways.

Fifth, *engage your heart*. The priest and the Levite saw the needy man. What made the Samaritan different was that he did more than see; he let himself feel compassion. If you can see a person in need but feel nothing, that's something to talk with God about. A cool head can be useful in a crisis, but a cold or numb heart is a sign that something inside is spiritually broken. Don't be afraid to be *moved* to do good, and if you don't feel moved, do good anyway until it becomes a habit.

SPREAD IT AROUND

Kindness is like a good virus—once it starts, it spreads. There's nothing Willie likes better than going up to Miss Willa these days and slipping her a little money. He's so happy to be able to do something for her the way she did something for him when he needed it.

Uncle Si and Aunt Christine moved into a new house recently. Aunt Christine mentioned to some people that she and her husband needed more help moving things into the house. There happened to be a group of Air Force pilots up from Florida, and they said, "Look, we're doing nothing; we'll help this lady." They had no idea who Aunt Christine was, because she's never been on *Duck Dynasty*®, but they volunteered to help a stranger.

Somebody said, "Do you know who she is?" and one of the pilots said, "It doesn't matter who she is. She needs some help, so we'll help her."

So they went out and tore the seats out of their vans to make room to move the stuff.

Then someone said, "You know, that's Uncle Si's wife."

They turned out to be big fans, and they said, "You mean we're going up to Si's house?" They were ecstatic. They got to take some pictures with Si and get some autographs, and Si got to thank them for their service to our country.

When you have a mind-set to be kind, you never know who you might be helping.

WHERE TO START?

We've looked at five of the values that our family is committed to. Now it's your turn. If faith isn't already at the center of your family's life, that's a good place to start. Having both parents on board is best, but Miss Kay proves that even one person can plant the seed of faith if he or she is willing to fight for the family in prayer and action. If you've never decided to follow Jesus as the Lord of your life, will you take that step now? Tell someone about your decision so they can celebrate with you.

If you're already a believer, are you willing to set an example in your family of trusting Jesus, no matter what?

What is one thing you can do to demonstrate that trust in the way you relate to your family?

Take prayer next. If you're the only believer in your family, find a friend to pray with you for your family. If there are two believing adults in the family, start planning time to pray together for your family. What will you ask God to do for your family? Be prepared to bang on God's door until He opens it.

Does your family have a habit of holding grudges against each other? If so, you can start to set a tone of forgiveness by making a list of things you've been holding against people in your family. If forgiveness is new to you, start by forgiving the small daily stuff and pray about the big things that seem hard to let go of.

What about kindness? Once you've begun to build a habit of prayer and a habit of forgiveness, mark a week on your calendar and look for something kind to do for someone in your family every day that week. Then push it out to the next week until kindness gets to be a routine for you. If that's hard for you, add kindness to the list of things you're praying for your family.

Once you're doing those things, you'll already have started to live a life of obedience to God. Is there any other area of obedience God is trying to draw your attention to?

Give yourself and your family time. Our family didn't become what it is today overnight. It started with a tiny seed, a seed of redonkulous faith. In the right soil, that seed can produce a crop that will take your breath away.

VIDEO
DISCUSSION GUIDE

SESSION 1
REDONKULOUS FAITH

1. Hebrews 11:1 defines faith as "confidence in what we hope for and assurance about what we do not see." What is something you have confidence about that you can't see, or that hasn't happened yet?

2. How did Jase express faith in God when he was fourteen? How did his actions require faith in what he couldn't see?

3. What are you confident is true about God? Why are you confident? (If you're not confident of anything about God, what leads to your lack of confidence?)

4. Do you boldly share your faith as Jase did? What encourages you to do that? Or what gets in the way?

5. Read Matthew 13:3–9, 18–23. How would you summarize what this parable is about?

6. How does each of these things affect your confidence in Jesus Christ?

   • Trouble or persecution

   • The worries of this life

   • Money or the lack of it

7. What do you think God would like you to do in response to this parable?

8. How would you like others in your group to pray for you with regard to redonkulous faith?

SESSION 2
RADICAL FORGIVENESS

1. How did the family deal with Jep's sin? Were you surprised in any ways by how they handled it? If so, how? If not, why not?

2. How did Phil deal with Alan's sin? Is it unforgiving to ask someone to stay away from the family as long as they cling to their sin? Why or why not?

3. When you were growing up, how did you learn to handle situations when people hurt or offended you?

4. What does it mean to forgive someone? Alan defines it as not using someone's sin to hurt them. Is that a helpful way for you to understand it? Is there anything you'd add?

5. Read Matthew 18:21–22. What do you think about forgiving others seventy-seven (or more) times? What are the pros and cons of doing that?

6. Read Matthew 18:23–35. In what ways are you like the servant who was forgiven the debt of ten thousand talents? How easy is it for you to identify with him? Why is that?

7. How does the end of the story (verses 34–35) affect you? Are you more motivated by the king's kindness at the beginning of the story or his harshness at the end?

8. Why do you think it's so important to God that we forgive others?

9. How would you like others in your group to pray for you with regard to radical forgiveness?

SESSION 3
RAVENOUS PRAYER

1. Why do you think people are so grateful to see the Robertson family praying together to thank God for their dinner?

2. What do you take away from Phil's story about praying for the young man in Memphis?

3. Read Luke 11:5–10. In what ways is God like the neighbor asleep at midnight? In what ways is God unlike him?

4. What point is Jesus making in this story?

5. How easy is it for you to be bold, shameless, audacious, and persistent in prayer? Why is that?

6. Have you ever prayed for something for a long time? What was that long process like for you? What has been the result so far?

7. In the video Phil says,

> What were they prepared for when they prayed unceasingly to God? They were prepared for the Creator of the cosmos to say no. See, you pray to God and you ask Him to bless you, your family, your children, your livelihood, your country, your world. Sometimes God says, "No, it's your responsibility to stand up and do what you've asked Me to do. Get up and go forth. Love Me. Love your neighbor."

How do you respond to the idea that God may answer your prayer with, "No, you stand up and do it"? Is that something you're prepared to hear from God? What would you do if He said that?

8. How does this discussion move you to pray now?

SESSION 4
REAL OBEDIENCE

1. How positive or negative a word is *obedience* for you? Why?

   ____ Very positive

   ____ Somewhat positive

   ____ Neither positive nor negative

   ____ Somewhat negative

   ____ Very negative

2. What reasons for obeying God did Si give in the video? What other reasons can you add?

3. What good came out of Si's trip to Germany? Has something good ever come of your obedience? Describe the good thing that happened.

4. Read Matthew 21:28–32. Does Jesus praise the first son's behavior? If so, how? If not, how does He view the first son?

5. Which son do you most identify with? (Or do you identify with neither or both?)

6. What are some reasons why people don't obey God? What reasons are people willing to admit? What reasons do they not admit?

7. Give some examples of things God asks us to do. How do these commands conflict with selfishness?

8. How would you like others in your group to pray for you with regard to obedience?

SESSION 5
ROWDY KINDNESS

1. What examples of kindness did Willie and Si give in the video? What was it about those actions that made them kind?

2. Give an example of a time when someone was kind to you. What makes that experience stick in your memory?

3. Read Luke 10:25–37. What is surprising about what the Samaritan does?

4. Have you ever been in the position of the injured man in the story who desperately needed to receive kindness? If so, how has that experience affected you? Or if you've never experienced that, has that lack of experience affected your willingness to go out of your way for others?

5. Why do you think Jesus made the story about "Which of these three do you think was a neighbor?" (verse 36), not about "Who is my neighbor?" (verse 29)?

6. What are the main barriers you face in being more consistently kind? What can you do to address those barriers?

7. How would you like others in your group to pray for you with regard to rowdy kindness?

Faith Commander Church-Wide Curriculum

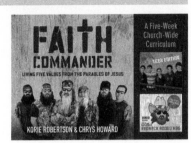

Living Five Family Values from the Parables of Jesus

Korie Robertson and Chrys Howard

Join the Robertson family of the hit television show, *Duck Dynasty®*, on an exciting ride through some of the Bible's most-loved parables. In this five-week, church-wide experience for all ages, you and your church will learn how to build a legacy of faith and apply faith-based values to every aspect of your life.

With their trademark humor and a whole bunch of adventure, the Robertson family will lead individuals, families, and whole churches through this five-session adventure.

The five sessions include:

1. Redonkulous Faith
2. Radical Forgiveness
3. Ravenous Prayer
4. Real Obedience
5. Rowdy Kindness

The *Faith Commander* Church Curriculum Kit contains the following:

- *Faith Commander* (book)
- *Faith Commander: A DVD Study*
- *Faith Commander Teen Edition* (book)
- *Faith Commander Teen Edition: A DVD Study*
- *Faith Commander Children's Curriculum* (with a Bonus *Willie's Redneck Rodeo VBS Curriculum*) on DVD-ROM
- *Willie's Redneck Rodeo VBS Director's Guide*
- *Faith Commander Getting Started Guide*

Available in stores and online!

ZONDERVAN®
.com